Table Of Contents

Forward

From $15,000 A Month To $184,000 A Month

Hi, this is Mike Filsaime. You've probably heard of my success with Butterfly Marketing but you've probably never heard of the secret strategist I had in my corner advising me on every move. His name is Rich Schefren.

Rich has been my business growth coach for more than a year. I've worked with him one on one and implemented his strategies.

From day one, Rich helped me plan and grow my internet business. His insights and questions caused me to stop and think. My business success didn't just happen; Rich helped me carve out a path that I've followed.

Before I met Rich, I was doing okay online; we made $15,000 a month. In May 2006, we banked $184,000 and that was not associated with any launch of a product. Those are the kinds of numbers I've grown accustomed to seeing after working with Rich.

Listen up. I've not only heard Rich's strategies, I've put them to use. There's a lot of junk floating around on the Internet – this is one of the exceptions. Put these strategies to work and prosper.

$3.1 Million Thanks

Hey. This is Harlan Kilstein, the direct response copywriter. I've known Rich Schefren since we both had hypnosis offices. Well, let me correct that – I had an office – he had a business. When I was making $5000 a week, Rich was making $145,000 a week. As I got to know Rich, I began to realize his success was no accident.

For 2 years, our offices were adjoining and I heard a "who's who" of the marketing world calling in to talk with Rich. In any given day Rich could be strategizing with Jay Abraham, Stephen Pierce, John Carlton, Alex Mandossian, Armand Morin, Jim Edwards, Yanik Silver, Rob Bell, Brad Fallon, Will Bonner, Jeff Paul, Mike Filsaime, or Carl Galletti. Even though these people are enormously successful, they pay attention to what he says.

From time to time, when I can catch a moment of his time, I've implemented many of his strategies myself. No matter where I think I am in understanding marketing, Rich is still light years ahead. I "guesstimate" that I've made over $3.1 million dollars listening to Rich's strategies. I urge you to do the same. I've read through Rich's manifesto and there's highlighting on every page. This report is not a sales letter; it's a gold mine.

The "Secrets" To Making It Big Online

What you now hold in your hands is just a snapshot of my two years of extensive research and testing with many of today's top offline and online marketers.

Up till now, this information has been closely held and only available to select online marketers who were accepted as clients to the Internet's most successful coaching program. Well known marketers Jim Edwards, Mike Filsaime, Brad Fallon, Tellman Knudson, (and many other top Internet marketing gurus who would prefer to remain anonymous) have paid upwards of $11,000 to have me remake, remodel and redesign their businesses.

I *strongly* suggest that you print this manifesto out right now, and read it immediately. Plus, there's a special chart on page 14 that I suggest you print out and hang near your workspace. There's a very big idea inside it and many people have made a fortune once they grasped the concepts you are about to receive right here for free.

Who Is Rich Schefren?

You might know me from the work I did with Jay Abraham, John Carlton, Jeff Paul, Stephen Pierce, Yanik Silver, Jeff Walker and Alex Mandossian.

Then about a year and a half ago, I disappeared from the limelight and began working on an elite level coaching program that has become quite famous in the upper-echelons of Internet marketing.

If you're an Online Marketing "insider," chances are you've heard who my clients are, and the phenomenal results they've been getting.

> **As Seen in**
> ## Early to Rise, Agora Publishing
>
> " Rich Schefren is arguably one of the world's best small-business strategists. His marketing strategies have been featured in the Wall Street Journal, and he's appeared on every major television network, including ABC, CBS, and NBC.
>
> Rich's business have done over $35 million in sales, and he currently coaches many of today's top internet gurus and service providers on streamlining their businesses whiles exploding their profits. "

I've been around for quite a while, yet I seem to be a mystery man to online marketers who aren't on the "inside". That's because, for the last 2 years, I've been the **"secret business coach"** working *behind the scenes* with Internet Marketing Gurus and multi-million dollar Internet businesses. Until recently, I purposely avoided the spotlight and *all* online publicity... despite being one of the world's most successful and sought after Internet business coaches.

I still feel awkward when I have to bring it up (and I tell you this only because it's important to help you understand how powerful the methods I am going to reveal to you are)... but my accomplishments have become somewhat *legendary*:

- At the age of 22 I took a failing clothing company from 1.5 million to 6.5 million in three years.

- At the age of 26 I started a hypnosis center that grew in to a 7.5 million dollar business in less than four years

- At the age of 31 I got involved in online marketing and within the first two years I generated over 4 million dollars in partnerships with Jay Abraham, John Carlton, Jeff Paul, Stephen Pierce, Yanik Silver, and Alex Mandossian.

- At the age of 33 I began working on a systemized coaching program whose members read like a who's who of the Internet (1shoppingcart, Jim Edwards, Mike Filsaime, Brad Fallon, Harlan Kilstein, Tellman Knudson, and many others I am not allowed to mention) and have averaged an increase of over 1.5 million dollars per member in the past 16 months.

I have also made millions in my own niche markets, as an online advisor and partner to Agora Publishing (a 250 million dollar information marketer), as a marketing partner to top poker professionals like Howard Lederer; and many other online activities that I prefer to still keep private.

Bottom line, I know how to build and grow systemized businesses and make money. I've been doing it for myself for the past 13 years, and for the past year and a half I've been coaching quite a few heavy hitters on how to do it my way.

Why Are These "Secrets" Being Shared?

I have already told you that for the past year and half I've been personally coaching some of the most successful online entrepreneurs, many of them you've probably heard of. What I didn't tell you yet was that it was all for a bigger purpose.

I went into coaching with a vision of the business I wanted to create. I wanted to create a system that could stand on its own (e.g. without me) and help experienced and rookie business owners re-engineer their strategy and systemize their processes, so they could multiply their profits while slashing the number of hours they worked.

Strategic Profits Coaching

A proven system that allows smart-but-overwhelmed business owners to quickly consolidate profitability, eliminate wasted effort, and put the best possible version of your business on autopilot. So you rake in more money, spend less time in the office (and more time on vacation)... while everything runs (and grows) with amazing professional efficiency.

I am now only a few months away from achieving my vision. But, I recently entered into a partnership that is going to force me to radically scale back the number of hours I dedicate to my coaching business. What this means is, aside from a select group of entrepreneurs, most online marketers may never get the chance to work with me personally ever again.

That's why I decided that it was time to get this information out there for everyone to benefit from.

The Reason Why Most Internet Marketers Struggle

I just got back from a recent Internet marketing conference. It was great seeing all the familiar faces, current clients and having the opportunity to make new friends. But every time I go to an Internet marketing event I am struck by how almost everybody in attendance is approaching their business or starting their business the wrong way.

Lack of fundamental business building knowledge is really the primary cause for so much struggling and time wasting, it's sad. It's the reason why the overwhelming majority of people new to the Internet will fail in achieving their dreams even if they buy lots of products, study them religiously and work extremely hard.

I'm going to address the issues I see, because I know from past experience that my unique perspective can really make a tremendous difference in your business, as it has for many of my coaching clients. I cannot sit on the sidelines anymore and allow so many dreams fall by the wayside due to a misunderstanding of how successful businesses are built.

This Manifesto will expose those issues, one by one, and you will gain clarity about your relationship to your business (and how to grow it) that you've never had before.

To kick things off, <u>I'm going to show you how my clients achieved an average increase of 1.5 million dollars in their businesses</u>, and I'm going to show you the some of the exact concepts that are responsible for this growth.

But first, let's take a look at where the Internet is today and put it in perspective with traditional business....

Putting The Internet Into Perspective

Before we dive into the growth strategies, we need to step back and put an Internet marketing business into perspective. You need to see how it fits into the larger world of "business." Looking at how traditional business evolves will give you some idea of where the current state of Internet marketing is, and how it's changing. Understanding the current state (maturity) of online business is critical to your long term success.

Now first of all, the Internet is heating up again. In fact, just this morning I watched a political show detailing how important the Internet will be to the 2008 presidential elections.

This means that more and more businesses are going to get a lot more serious about the Internet. Last week I spent a few days with Agora Publishing (the 250 million dollar a year Info-marketing powerhouse) planning a new project which I will be telling you about a little later in this Manifesto. When I walked into their offices I was invited to sit in on a meeting that was already in progress. The meeting had five of their top people strategizing their marketing plan of attack for the next two weeks in a highly competitive niche. The plan was simple yet powerful; it played to their strengths, and will likely put a few of the smaller players who are currently marketing in that niche out of business. I was relieved that I was not operating in that particular segment.

All of this reminded me of a slide I have used in a number of the presentations that I have done over the past year or so.

If you've seen me speak, perhaps, you remember it?

Why you need to build an INTERNET BUSINESS

The internet is still wild west days... but just like every other industry and media channel sooner or later businesses will smother the self-employed.

examples

The Infomercial Business

The Auto Industry- over 250 Car Companies in the 1900's

The cable TV industry

The newspaper industry

When I flash this slide on the screen, I tell people that if they haven't built an actual business around what it is they are currently doing they ought to strongly consider creating one today, ASAP!

The reason is that big business always "beats up" and steals the lunch money of the small independent operators. And if you know anything about business or have witnessed the birth or growth of any industry you have already seen the pattern play out time and time again.

My own experience confirms this big business effect too. During my 4 years in the clothing business, taking a 1.5 million dollar a year business to over 6.5 million dollars a year, I saw first hand the way big business boxes out the smaller guys. My store was on Broadway in lower Manhattan. At the time the street was full of independent retailers with their own unique stores – fast forward four years later and the rents had skyrocketed forcing the little players out of business and <u>the invasion of the big time mall stores was in full effect</u>.

When I approached the hypnosis market I built my business into the largest that had ever existed and easily put hundreds of smaller independent hypnotists right out of business. <u>We were spending about 3 million dollars a year on advertising and my small time competitors could hardly afford to spend a few thousand. Once again proving business beats the little guy</u>.

My good friend, John Carlton, tells me stories about his early days in the infomercial business and how they would shoot the commercial during the day (guerilla video style) and air it at night for free. If it sold, they would keep running it, if it didn't they would shoot a new video the very next day.

Today if you wanted to compete in the infomercial business, you better step up to the plate with seven figures and be willing to lose it all. You want to know why? Because the industry matured and the original entrepreneurs who approached the infomercial business as a business were successful and continued to grow until they completely changed the industry. Companies like Guthy-Renker, who used to be an audio-tape manufacturer, became a $750,000,000 a year company because they treated the infomercial opportunity as a business.

Time Is Running Out, But You Can Still Build A Wildly Successful Online Business

The reason I mention all this is that when John Carlton told me about the early days of the infomercial business, he could've just as easily been talking about the current state of Internet marketing.

Find a niche, throw up a page, get some pay per click traffic, and if it works continue to develop it, if not, find another niche. Sounds familiar, doesn't it?

Listen, more and more successful offline companies are coming online everyday. Practically every week, my office receives several calls from business that are successful offline that want to bring their niche marketing online. You also have very successful direct response companies that have already made the transition to the online world (like Agora) that are continually looking for new niches where they can point their deep resources of talent. And if that wasn't enough, you've also got people who are actually consumers in the niche who are looking at the online environment thinking they could build their dream business around their passion. Oh yes, let's not forget you also have all the other Internet marketers who are looking for hot niches, too. This means there are an awful lot of people out there looking to take your lunch money!

But before I go any further, I want to share what a shoplifting prevention expert once shared with me when I was in the clothing business. He told me that the sensors on the clothing and the guards roaming around the store were not really about catching shoplifters, it was to make your store less appealing than other stores to shoplift in. In other words, you want to have more security than the others around you – so would be shoplifters will go where it's easiest to steal.

Ultimately you want to create the same effect in the niche that you operate in. You should build a business that works so well, where you have enough products it makes competing with you undesirable. Sophisticated competitors will understand that you could take your front end products and give them away free, or with a 100% affiliate commission, and it wouldn't affect your income because you would still have back-ends, cross-sells and upsells.

And the good news is that you *still* have time. The Internet is still somewhat like the Wild West, and you can still stake out your niche and build a real business in it, but I promise you the opportunity won't last forever.

Now let's look at a few obstacles that currently stand in your way...

Obstacles To Achieving Your Business Success

Now that you know how the Internet is evolving, and that you should be focused on building a real business, let's take a look at the obstacles you might face in actually creating a real business that has staying power.

By exposing and eliminating these problems, you'll be able to grow your business faster (and easier) than you ever thought possible. These are the same overriding concepts that ultra-wealthy business builders understand and operate on.

The format of this section will be similar to a medical diagnosis. You'll see the problem, its symptoms, cause and an overview of the solution.

Let's take a look at one fundamental problem most Internet marketers' experience.

Symptoms: Buying anything that looks like it'll make you money, getting no results.
Cause: Opportunistic thinking
Internet Business Problem: Lack of Strategy

The very first obstacle we need to look at is you and your thinking.

The way I see things is that there are two different diametrically opposing ways of thinking when it comes to building a business and making money online. There's opportunistic thinking and strategic thinking. The slide below is from one of the first presentations from my elite coaching program.

Opportunistic vs. Strategic

Opportunistic	Strategic
An opportunity arises and you grab it.	You have an end in mind, a vision.
Most business owners who struggle, are busy with the day to day of their business and take action on what's appealing.	Successful entrepreneurs know their vision, develop different alternatives for its accomplishment, and choose the approach they think is most probable. They continually ask "what are my best opportunities to achieve my vision?"

Here's the deal, opportunity seekers think opportunistically and entrepreneurs think strategically.

An opportunity seeker is always looking for their big opportunity to make lots of money from the hot opportunity of the moment. Their only criteria is, "Can I make money from this?" So today it's Adsense, tomorrow it something else, and yesterday it was some other hot concept already forgotten. Opportunity seekers buy lots of products, and they use only a few of them, and the ones they do use get abandoned when the next so-called "easy" way to make money comes by. The question they ask themselves is, "What's the easiest way for me to make money right now?"

A true entrepreneur, on the other hand, is a completely different animal altogether. An entrepreneur has a clear vision of what they want the business to become. Because they have a vision they can analyze their own strengths, their competitor strengths, the marketplace preferences and devise different strategies for achieving their vision. After reviewing the pros and cons of each strategic alternative they pick the one strategy most certain to successfully achieve their vision. The entrepreneur knows that their biggest opportunity is always inside their business, following their ideal strategy and not the hot product that everyone is mailing for this week.

And here's some inside information that any seasoned direct marketer will confirm. It's about 100 times easier to sell to an opportunity seeker than it is an entrepreneur. Why? Because the opportunity seeker has no criteria – if you can convince him or her that they can make money with it, you've made your sale. An entrepreneur, on the other hand, has to compare what you are offering to their current plans – will it make it easier for them to achieve their vision? Is this something that fits into their current approach and if it does is it superior to what they are currently doing?

And here's the rub, the overwhelming majority of Internet marketers are nothing more than digital opportunity seekers. They have no strategy, they hop from one approach to another, and while they may have some arbitrary income goal they have no vision of the business they would need to create in order to achieve it. And since they don't have a clear vision they can not follow any sort of detailed plan to accomplish it. So they end up buying anything and everything that comes with a big promise of easy money with the hope that this is going to be it – this is their big chance to make it big. They especially love (and fall victim to) the "Business in a box" products where the promises are huge rewards with little to no effort.

Alright, let's say that I have either convinced you that you need to be an entrepreneur and build a business, or you already knew it. Now, let's talk about what will stand in your way....

Poor Business Design Results In You Doing All The Work

Below you will see that I've broken up the traditional Internet business into twelve critical areas. All of them are important, wouldn't you agree?

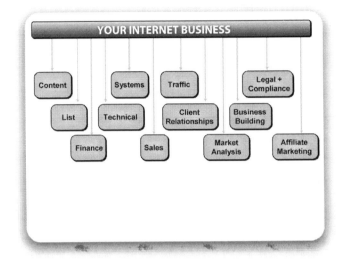

But we can dive a lot deeper into an Internet business can't we? It's not so simple.

We can break out each of these areas into smaller functions – the actual stuff that needs to get done.

Let's take a look at what each of these activities consists of...

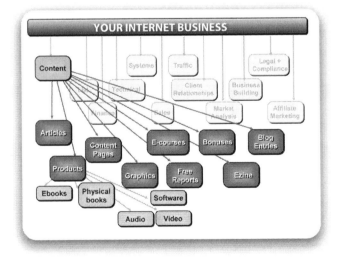

Content activities include:
- Articles
- Products
- eBooks & physical books
- Audio & Video
- Software
- Content pages for SEO
- Graphics
- Free reports & eCourses
- eZines
- Bonuses
- Blog Posts & Podcasts

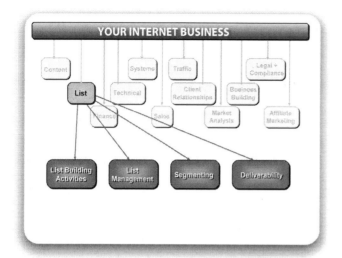

List activities include:

- List building tactics
- List management
- Segmenting
- Deliverability

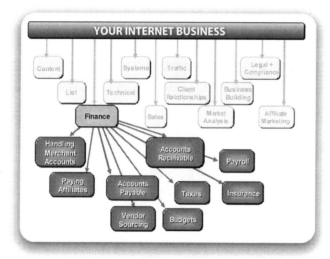

Finance activities include:

- Merchant accounts
- Paying affiliates
- Accounts payable
- Vendor sourcing
- Budgets
- Taxes
- Insurance
- Payroll
- Accounts receivable

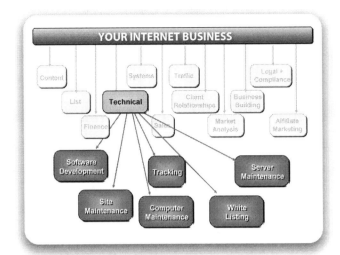

Technical activities include:

- Software development
- Site maintenance
- Computer maintenance
- Tracking
- White listing
- Server maintenance

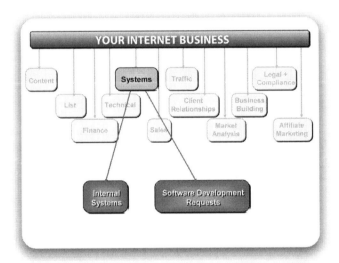

Systems activities include:

- Internal systems
- Software development
  (If you're trying to build your own business, at times you want to create your own software to automate recurring tasks)

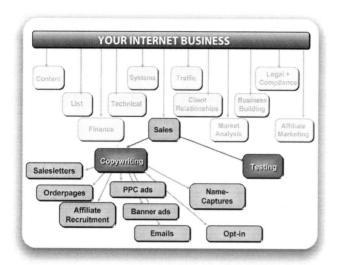

Copywriting activities include:
- Sales letters
- Order pages
- Affiliate recruitment
- Pay-per-click
- Banner ads
- Emails
- Opt-ins
- Name captures
- Testing

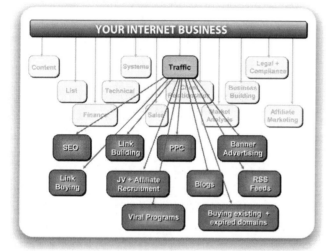

Traffic activities include:
- SEO
- Link buying
- Link building
- JV recruitment
- Viral programs
- Pay-per-click
- Blogs
- Buying an existing and expired domains
- RSS feeds
- Banner advertising

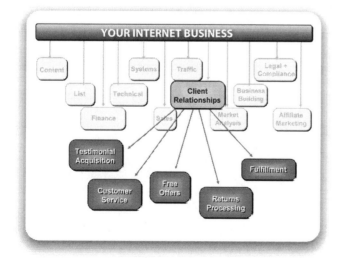

Client relationships activities:
- Getting testimonials
- Customer service
- Free offers
- Return processing
- Fulfillment

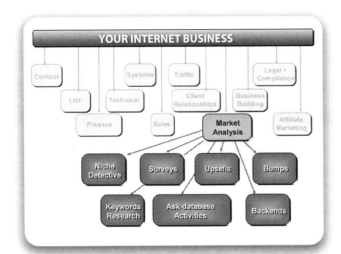

Marketing analysis includes
- Niche detective
- Surveys
- Keyword research
- Ask database
- Up-sales
- Backends
- Bumps

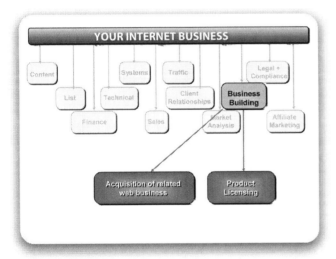

Business building activities:
- Acquisition potentially of related Web sites
- Buying competitors or buying similar Web sites
- Buying sites offering what people would buy before or after they buy your product.
- Product licensing

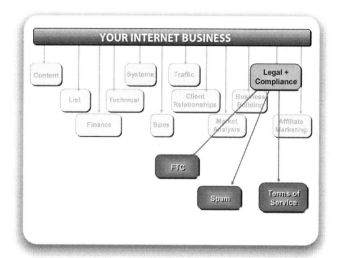

Legal and compliances:

- FTC Regulation
- SPAM issues
- Terms of service
- Business licenses
- IRS filings

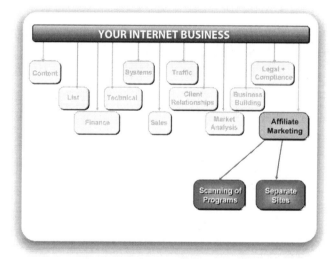

Affiliate marketing activities:

- Scanning of programs
- Figuring out which affiliate programs you should be a member of so that you can promote other people's products
- Developing separate sites to promote other people's products so you can build a better list for your own product...

And after breaking out all the activities that need to take place in your Internet business (and by no means is this breakout supposed to be exhaustive) you are left with a business model that is quite ridiculous.

If you're ready to see what this business model really looks like, go ahead and turn the page (but brace yourself)....

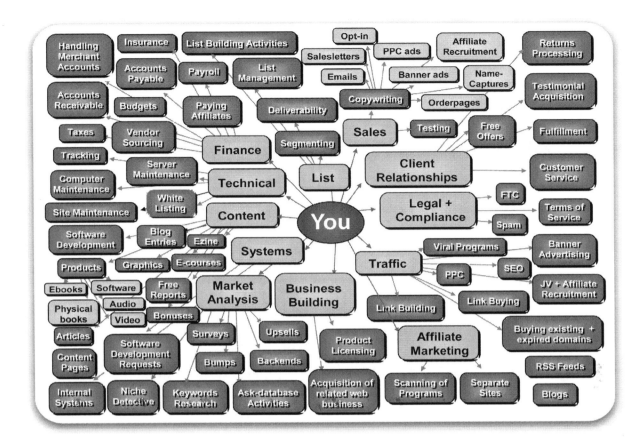

Now, isn't that ridiculous?

Frustration, Hard Work And Marginal Results

If you've ever been frustrated with your progress, overwhelmed with the amount of work you need to get done, or just plain tired – is there any wonder why? Seriously, even if you were to outsource it all – don't you see that you couldn't even manage all the outsourcers that would be required to get all this work done?

And here's the really crazy part, even though this is the model that most Internet marketers are following, do you know what they spend an overwhelming amount of time on? Searching for more activities, tactics, and tricks to squeeze in to the chart above...it's crazy isn't it? Why on earth would you spend any more time looking for more to do? You aren't even getting done all the stuff you already want to get done – but most Internet marketers are on the lookout for the latest and greatest opportunity to add to their list of stuff that isn't going to get done. Make no mistake: the chart above is the chart of a person who is sadly lacking in strategy. It screams OPPORTUNIST!

So here's my question to you...

Since when is
MORE
the solution to having
TOO MUCH?

The solution to having too much is not to go get more – If you were to look at your behavior, wouldn't you agree that you've been subconsciously following the plan of adding more and more tactics and activities to your list of 'things to do'?

Let me clue you in on a small piece of advice. As long as your organizational chart looks like the one below, you'll always be spinning your wheels wondering why you are not achieving the level of success you've always wanted.

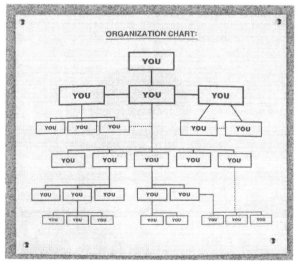

Now, before you jump to the conclusion that I am recommending you hire some people; recognize the problem with Internet marketing goes much deeper than that.

I've only peeled back the first few layers of this onion; if you really want to get at the truth we are going to have to get a little more personal.

Playing "Simon Says" Is Not A Business Strategy

Let's return to our previous conversation about strategy. My big question to you is: Do you have a strategy?

I came up with the slide below after a late night conversation with one of my closest friends and frequent partner on projects, Stephen Pierce. We were talking about business strategy and the lack of it in the Internet marketing space. And Stephen pointed out that almost everybody's strategy was to do the same as everyone else, but just try to do it a little better.

sameness
sameness
sameness
sameness

The predominant internet and small business strategy is just doing the same thing as everyone else, only doing it longer, faster, and smarter than everyone else...

It was a great observation for two very important reasons: the first reason is that it's true and the second is that this is not a strategy at all; it's simply the opportunist motto.

And it's this type of thinking that reinforces all the issues we've already surfaced earlier.

This, my friend is not an entrepreneur's strategy, it's the way Lemmings die.

Don't worry though, the problem is not hopeless – actually if you identify with anything you've read so far you should feel a sense of relief, because the truth is you've been working harder than you need to for a fraction of the results you deserve. And it's not your fault – because no one is really talking about this.

I had fallen victim to this same line of thinking myself, and I should have known better. Before I got on the Internet I built, ran, and owned several successful multi-million dollar companies with upwards of 100 employees and yet I got swept up in this backwards business thinking too.

I spent my first two years online following the same line of thinking I've just laid out for you. Even though during that time I worked with Jay Abraham, John Carlton, Jeff Paul, Yanik Silver, Alex Mandossian, Stephen Pierce and many others; I was frustrated, overwhelmed and exhausted. I was truly acting like an opportunist mistakenly believing I was being strategic. Sure, I made good money (although it was less than I had been making in my offline businesses) but I was working much harder than I ever had.

When I finally realized the error of my ways it was like waking up from a two year fog, and immediately my business and my life began to change for the better. It made such a profound difference for me; I knew I needed to share it with others. The first time was at a Jay Abraham seminar – when I was done presenting, I was surrounded by people telling me the 90 minutes were the most important 90 minutes of their business life, and that this was the information that they were missing. One very successful woman was crying when she told me her and her husband needed to hear what I just said so badly that I had saved their lives!

Why Even Gurus Listen Closely To What I Have To Say

I then spent the next six months documenting and refining everything that needed to be done to strategize, streamline and systemize a business. When I was through I began a pilot coaching program where I accepted twenty five Internet marketers as clients and the results have been nothing less than spectacular.

In the first eight months alone, my clients increased their businesses by 30 million dollars. In the next eight months they grew another 7 million dollars, and the numbers continue to climb. But the huge income increases tell only *half* the story because the average number of hours worked also plummeted. Two coaching clients who never took time off before, had enough free time on their hands they bought boats, which they now enjoy in their free time. One client who hadn't taken a long weekend in over five years already took three months off this year and is planning on taking the entire summer off too. All the while their profits continued to soar!

Even though the results were mind-blowing, I knew I could make the program even better, so once again I spent six months reworking the material. Four months ago I finished, so I started a second group a few months ago – this time limiting the group to 40 clients. And the staggering results are starting to come in from this group as well.

(You might be wondering why I limited the number of coaching clients both times I have accepted applications. Well, one of the reasons is that unlike most programs out there that call themselves coaching programs but are really group coaching programs, I get on the phone personally with each and every client, each and every month, for a half hour call).

But I am getting way ahead of myself here. I still have more I want to share with you. So, back to the purpose of this Manifesto, your Internet business.

Do You Know What An Hour Of Your Time Is Worth?

I don't mean to get all philosophical on you, but have you ever really thought about your time – it's your life. If you really think about it, time is all you have. Moreover, there's no such thing as free time. You can't save free time and use it later. You have leisure time but it's not free time. When you waste time in front of your computer mindlessly surfing and then rationalizing to yourself that you were just using some of your free time – you actually just wasted some of your life. It's not leisure time unless that is what you're choosing to do above all other activities; all other activities like going swimming, going on vacation, spending time with your family, friends or on your hobbies.

I've been told that Dan Kennedy has a countdown clock in his home office that goes in reverse, letting him know how many minutes, hours, and days he has left just so he's constantly reminded that he's only got a limited amount of time on this planet and that there's no free time, because the countdown never stops. (I'll be speaking at Dan's next information marketing seminar in November, if you are coming, make sure to introduce yourself and let me know what you thought of this Manifesto).

Alright, so what's this got to do with your Internet business? EVERYTHING!

The reason you are not making the kind of money in your business or working the amount of hours you want is that you have not made it a point to continually increase the worth of your time. Let me be redundant here for the sake of clarity...

All time has value; and the way you think about time and think about yourself will affect everything that happens to you inside and outside your business for the rest of your life. In short, you have to value your time before anyone else will.

I'm always shocked at how many people don't have any idea what the value of their time is, or how to increase the value of their time. So, the question is, "what is your time worth?" Do you know what your time is worth? Do you know what your time needs to be worth to achieve your income goals?

If you don't know what your time is worth and what it needs to be worth, then you can not make effective decisions on what activities you should be spending your time on and what activities you should have others do for you.

So, let's roll up our sleeves and figure out together what the value of your time needs to be to get you where you want to be.

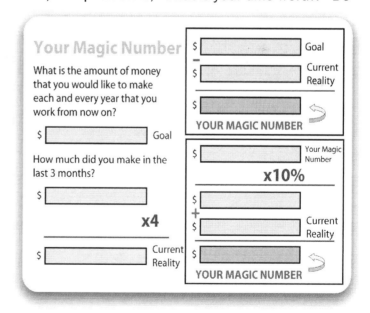

I was fortunate enough to attend John Reese's solo-seminar back in March of 2004. At some point within the first few hours John told us to take our income goal and subtract what we were making from it, and then take 10% of the difference and add that back to what we are currently making as our short term goal. It was genius in its simplicity. I've created a slide to walk you through this process because it forms the basis of the time calculations we are going to do together.

In the first box on the left you enter the amount of money you always dreamed you would make when owning your own business.

In the box below that one, enter in the amount you made in the past three months.

And the bottom box is your income for the past three months multiplied by four to get what you are currently on track to make.

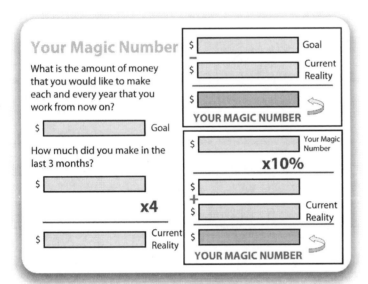

Now you simply subtract the amount you are on track to make (your current reality) from the amount you always wanted to make. And you are left with your magic number which is the amount you need to increase your income to reach your goal.

Next, you multiply your magic number by 0.1 and then add it to what you are currently making. You end up with your income target, used next.

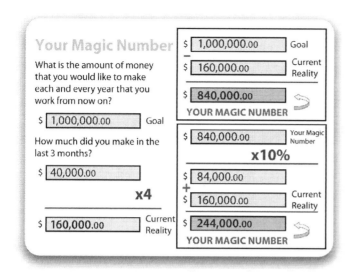

In case you are confused, here's an example. If you follow along then you can see the income goal is 1 million dollars a year, and that this person made 40k in the past 3 months which means he's trending toward 160k annually. We subtract the 160k he's making from the million he wants to make and you can see he's 840k short. So, we take 10% of the 840K and we get 84K. We add the 84K to the 160K he's on track to make and our new short term goal is 244K.

Alright, so you now have a new financial target to get to. How can you do it? You need to make some changes if you are going to get there, and what you need to do is change the amount of money you are able to generate per hour worked.

The Difference Between Productive And Wasted Time

Let's Find Out Together
WHAT YOUR TIME IS WORTH

How much do you want to earn in the next 12 months? $_____

How many days a week do you work? _____

How many hours a day do you work? _____

How many productive hours a day do you work? _____

How many productive hours a week do you work? _____

How many weeks per year do you work? _____

Total hours available to you right now to produce desired income: _____

What you must generate an hour: $_____

Divide by 60 to get your minute rate: $_____

The chart on the left is going to give you greater clarity about the value of your time than you have ever had before.

On the first line enter the amount you arrived at in the previous slide (your current step). Then fill out the number of days a week you work and the number of hours per day you work.

So what is productive time?

Before I answer the question, let me tell you about a tip I got from a good friend of mine. I was talking to Alex Mandossian one afternoon and I remarked at how impressed I was with his output, and how envious I was. And he said "Rich, what you need to do is go out and get a kitchen timer and set it for 60 minutes and then just work on building profit during those 60 minutes – nothing else." Let me tell you, at first it wasn't easy – I got thirsty and wanted to get some water, I had the urge to go online and check my stats, I had to go to the bathroom, and there were all these little interruptions. But eventually I was able to go a complete hour full throttle on nothing but profit building activities. And that my friend is what productive time is all about.

Productive time is time directly generated to income. So what percentage of the time are you productive? Before you answer, consider this: One study of Fortune 500 CEOs estimated they had 28 productive minutes a day. Another one estimated it at 38 productive minutes a day.

I know, it sounds crazy, right? Only 28 or 38 minutes a day? But think about what a CEO does and how much time they actually get to focus on profit building activities. Since you don't have the same level of responsibilities as a Fortune 500 CEO you can have a lot more productive time. But productive time doesn't appear like magic, you have to be focused and disciplined.

Here are some examples of non-productive time; talking to friends, surfing the Internet, checking and reading email, answering your phone, studying and learning time, checking Web site stats, organizing your desk, and cleaning your office.

Reading an eBook, even if it reveals the most powerful secrets on making money that have ever been discovered, is not productive time. It only gets productive time when you actually do the work, or you leverage someone else to do it. This is a very important distinction because so many opportunity seekers confuse learning with earning. New knowledge has no worth to your business unless it's implemented and acted upon.

How Many Productive Hours a Day DO YOU WORK?

What percentage of the time are you productive?

One study of fortune 500 CEOs estimated it at 28 productive minutes a day. Another one estimated 38 productive minutes a day.

Productive time = time directly generating income.

Non-Productive Time	Productive Time	Super Productive Time
• Talking to friends • Surfing the internet • Checking & reading email • Answering your phone(s) • Studying & learning time • Checking website stats • Organizing your desk • Cleaning your office	• Creating products • Marketing products • Managing $$$ projects • Creating scale	• Creating systems that create products • Creating systems that market products • Creating systems that build scale

Of course, I'm not suggesting that you shouldn't spend any time on these activities. You need to spend time learning, and you do need to talk to your friends. I'm simply pointing out that this is not what we would consider productive time. These activities are maintenance. This is what you have to do. But you cannot consider the time as productive time because it doesn't build a business, it doesn't increase your income, it's just there. You have to do it, that's part of life.

Productive time is time spent creating products, marketing products, improving your marketing process, managing money making projects, setting up joint venture deals, and creating scalability in your business.

But there is even something more profitable and strategic than productive time, I call it super-productive time.

<u>Super-productive time is when you create a system around any of your money making activities. Examples of super-productive time would be: creating systems that create products and creating systems that market products.</u>

When I was focused on niche marketing I developed a product development and marketing system for eBooks. Everything from keyword research to buying pay per click traffic was done by someone other than me, and here's the point I was not involved at all once I had the system working. In other words the researcher did the keyword research, she then forwarded it to the webmaster and the ghostwriter, the webmaster registered the domain and put page up with keywords as placeholders, while the ghostwriter wrote the book, the salesletter, the name capture, etc...

New products were developed each and every month – no matter what. The business continued to grow whether I worked a day that month or not – and that is why the time you invest in creating income producing systems is super-productive time.

Let's Find Out Together
WHAT YOUR TIME IS WORTH

How much do you want to earn in the next 12 months? $ 250,000

How many days a week do you work? 6

How many hours a day do you work? 10

How many productive hours a day do you work? 2

How many productive hours a week do you work? 12

How many weeks per year do you work? 50

Total hours available to you right now to produce desired income: 600

What you must generate an hour: $ 416.66

Divide by 60 to get your minute rate: $ 6.95

Alright, I think that's more than enough explaining, let's get back to you and the number of productive and super productive hours you have a day. Do you have an hour of productive time a day? 2 hours? What's your most conservative estimate at this point?

Unless you have really focused on maximizing your productive time before, I wouldn't think that you have more than 2 hours of productive time a day. Remember, we are talking about income generating activities only!

I have completed the entire slide so that you can see how this whole process works.

Here we have the next step goal of making $250,000 annually. We work 6 days a week and spend approximately 10 hours a day in our office or in front of our computer. We have estimated we are able to squeeze out 2 hours a day of productive time. This leaves us with 12 hours a week completely focused on building revenue. Multiply the 12 hours by 50 weeks and we have 600 hours a year to achieve our goal of $250,000. This means that we have to generate an average $416.66 of net income for each productive hour that we have. Or more to the point you need to make $833.22 each day six days a week, fifty weeks a year.

The Easiest Way To Boost Your Hourly Rate

If you are asking yourself "how in the hell could I achieve my hourly rate, everyday?" the answer will not be found in an eBook or a home study course. The answer is that you need to build a scalable business that provides you, the business owner, with the maximum amount leverage possible.

That's why knowing your hourly rate is so important. It exposes you, maybe for the first time, to the reason why you aren't making the kind of money you always dreamed about. And the answer is your business is not currently set up to help you achieve and then surpass your hourly rate!

The next reason you need to know your hourly rate is it serves as the barometer for which activities you should personally be spending your time on and which activities you should be outsourcing. The trick is to consistently focus on those activities that can raise your hourly rate. Start delegating and outsourcing what needs to be done that costs you less than the hourly rate you need to generate.

So, we've just surfaced two concepts crucial to raising your hourly rate - scalability and effectively outsourcing. Let's take a look at scalability first.

Using Leverage & Scalability Can Make You Wealthy

Creating Scale in Your Business

· If you are unsure about how to generate profits over your hourly rate usually you have a leverage problem not a knowledge problem.

· You increase leverage by:
1. Isolating activities that generate more income than it costs to get it done.
2. Increasing one or more of the variables of any of the profit producing formulas.
3. Developing and implementing a business plan that creates leverage through a tight focus and the proper strategy.

In my coaching program I spend a considerable amount of time focused on building up the leverage and scalability of your business. Unfortunately I don't have the space or time to go into great detail here, but I can certainly get you started.

Take a look at the slide on the left – the first point is that most people never get close to making their hourly rate because they mistakenly believe that what's keeping them from earning that kind of money is missing knowledge. And while there might be an element of truth to the missing knowledge theory, it's really only applicable if you are brand new to the Internet and have very limited marketing knowledge. If you don't fall into that category then knowledge is not your primary problem.

To illustrate my point about building leverage into your business, here's a story that we'll build off of.

During my junior year in college two of the classes I took were philosophy and comparative literature. Now, I don't remember all the details but for both classes the biggest portion of our grade was based on our final papers. And since there was some overlap in the two courses I figured out a way to write one paper for both. I was then able to spend more time on the one paper (but less than I would have spent on two) and ended up with a 4.0 in both classes with less work then would have originally been required.

Are you with me so far?

The goal in school – get good grades, the goal in business – increase profits. Anything that makes your current business activities more profitable without more work is increasing your leverage.

The Concept Of Working Less And Making More

If you are getting this you should see that you want the work you do in your business to serve you in as many ways as possible. <u>You do this by sticking to **one** niche, developing a full funnel of products, and instituting cross-sell, upsells, and back-ends to your audience.</u>

By continually working in that one niche – every successive product you rollout becomes more and more profitable. This means that your leverage continues to get bigger and bigger. Let's say that you get 1000 customers and 100 affiliates from your first product, when you launch your second product you already have a list of customers to make an offer to and you have your original 100 affiliates to grow from. In addition, any new customers you get from your second product might be impressed enough that they want more of what you have to offer so they search and find your first product and they buy that too. And so on, and so on, and so on.

This is creating scalability and leverage in a nutshell. Obviously there are much more advanced methodologies and strategies, but if you are not tightly focused then all the advanced stuff won't do you any good.

<u>The bottom line is that if you can't earn your hourly rate right now – you've got to get focused so you can start gaining more and more leverage. Nothing else is more important. Period.</u>

The Real Difference Between Outsourcing And Out-tasking

In order to be successful online you simply must learn how to outsource effectively. Unfortunately most people are approaching outsourcing all wrong. Their flawed thinking begins with the very first question that they ask themselves when considering outsourcing. Most struggling Internet entrepreneurs ask themselves: **"Where or how can I get this done the cheapest?"**

The answer to the above question leads to a lot of disappointment, frustration, missed opportunities and heartache. The reason why is that it displays a deep level of ignorance about what makes a business successful. Frankly, the question borderlines on the absurd...

First off, it's the wrong question because <u>the cheapest outsourcing solution is almost never the most reliable, or the quickest, or the most knowledgeable, or the best choice.</u> When all is said and done, the old saying that you get what you pay for is really true. And since we've already established that your time has value – when you waste it by having to continually spend time on the activity even though you outsourced it, it costs you a great deal more than you might think.

In an interview with Armand Morin last year I talked about the difference between out-tasking and outsourcing. I was surprised by the number of people who have followed up with me who wanted to thank me for this one distinction.

Which Question Are You Asking Yourself When You Consider Outsourcing?

When you ask the question "where or how can I can this done the cheapest?" you are taking an out-tasking approach. Your focus is on getting the activity done. When you take this approach you are forced to continually go through the selection process each and every time you need the job done. I call this outsourcing turnover, which when you consider the total amount of time you dedicate to finding and selecting a person it is quite expensive. What makes this approach even worse is that there is always a greater risk in dealing with a new outsourcer than an outsourcer that has a track record of delivering as promised.

Outsourcing is about developing long term relationships with people who have expertise outside your own. The better question is "How can I maintain access to a talented person who can do _____ on a long term basis, so we can seize on opportunities as they present themselves and be assured a quality job?" When you take this approach you end up building a team of independent professionals on call for your next business conquest. Over time, you and your team work better and better together and it's your company that reaps most of the benefits.

Some of my clients have begun to offer a 25% bonus in their postings on outsourced projects when they come in on time, as expected, without a lot of help from them. And I've been told by each and every one of them that they thought it was money very well spent.

Now we're going to look at a way to make your business and your outsourcing relationships ten times more profitable. But first, I have some bad news...

How To Make Your Business And Your Outsourcing Relationships 10X More Profitable

The bad news is; Even when you purposefully engineer outsourcing relationships things can still go wrong.

Pay very close attention to the problems on the left. My experience has shown these three causes are responsible for a lot more than just outsourcing challenges. In fact, being deficient in any one of these three skill sets will certainly stunt your business growth.

Since each of these skills are so vital to your success let's take a look at each outsourcing issue individually.

There are two ways that work should be done inside your business; systems and projects.

If it's an activity that's ongoing, or something that is done more than once you should develop a systemized way of doing it inside your business.

If it's temporary, goal directed, has a beginning and an end, and is unique it should be managed as a project.

It's surprising to me that I've never heard anyone else talk about this distinction (between systems and projects) because that's really what entrepreneurship is all about. Being an entrepreneur is about developing, installing, and continually improving the systems inside your business while also being involved in a limited number of projects.

the **2** ways work should be done in your business

Systems & Projects

You're An Untrained Project Manager Managing Projects!

Project management is a very important skill for the entrepreneur. Yet, most if not all the entrepreneurs I meet are untrained project managers, managing projects. Think about how absurd that is. My advice to you is if you're managing projects, it would be a very good idea to develop your project management skills. That's why I teach project management to every client I have because it's that important.

How Work Should Be Done Inside & Outside Your Business

The next cause that Forrester Research identified for outsourcing challenges is "The lack of a good process for specifying the work". This is also an obstacle to getting more leverage in your business, and the reason why entrepreneurs struggle with systemizing their business.

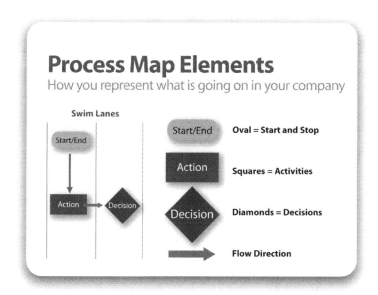

One of the best ways to document the way work should be done and how it interrelates to other activities inside your business is by process mapping.

Edward Deming, the father of the quality movement and the man responsible for Japan's rise after World War II said "If you can't describe what you're doing as a process, you don't know what you're doing." I couldn't agree more.

The good news is that process mapping is really simple. There are only 4 different elements to a process map - That's it! The oval represents the start and end so you really only use that twice. The arrows just show you the direction. So you're left with just two symbols to use; an action symbol or a decision symbol. The beauty of this is anything that you do can be reduced down to its core using this method.

One reason why process maps are a really important tool is that it makes it very easy to optimize the way you do things inside your business. The first time you do any activity inside your business it's generally not done the best way it can be.

When you start drawing your process map, it's really easy to see why your current way of doing an activity is less than ideal; more importantly you'll see where it can easily be improved upon. Looking at a process in a visual way makes it's easier to understand the flow, the interactions, and the sub-processes and sub-activities that are constraining your performance.

Listen, it's impossible to achieve optimum performance inside your business with flawed processes. Quality experts tell us 94 percent of any breakdown inside a business is due to faulty processes, not human problems, not anything else, it's a breakdown in a process. That's why having a tool as powerful as process mapping is crucial to streamlining your current operation.

In my company we process map everything we do, this allows us to easily train others, to outsource functions easily, and to continually improve our overall performance.

Here's an example of a process map from my company. It's a little outdated now, (meaning we don't use this process anymore) but the fundamentals are here for you to learn from.

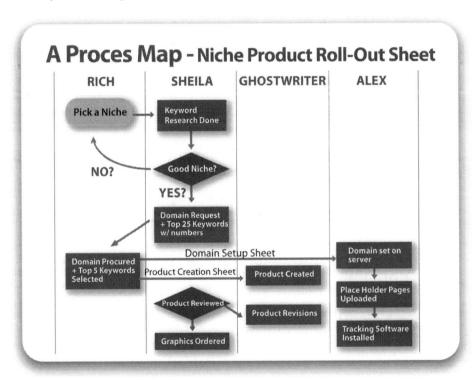

Do you see how easy it is to understand what is going on? And if you are any of the 4 people who are responsible for activities on this map, do you see how easy it is to understand how the activities you are responsible for relates to the entire process? Lastly, do you see how easy it is to understand who gets what from whom?

If you answered yes to the above questions you should begin process mapping.

Let us press on…

Metrics: The Language Of Business (And Profits)

Forrester Research lists the last cause for outsourcing challenges as not having the right metrics for measuring performance. Most marketers online understand website metrics but don't fully appreciate how easy it is to rate your current performance, spot opportunities, and effectively manage your business ,as well as your outsourcing relationships ,through metrics.

Let's look at using metrics for outsourcing. When developing an outsourcing relationship it's a good idea to use a Service Level Agreement (SLA). Basically it's an agreement between your business and the outsourcer about how performance will be measured (the metrics) and what the minimum acceptable levels of service are. Most online entrepreneurs don't do this and therefore they never share with the outsourcer how their work is going to be evaluated, which leads to substandard results.

The metrics vary considerably based on the process being outsourced, but here are a few guidelines to follow when choosing and developing your metrics:

- Be inline with the goal of the processes
- Motivate the 'right' behavior
- Be actionable and objective
- Not be too difficult to determine

Obviously, there's a lot more to metrics, but if you just start thinking about what metrics you could use to judge your own performance as well as your outsourcing relationships you'll be light years ahead of where most online marketers are today.

A Quick Recap Of Online Business Building Principles

What I've attempted to do in this manifesto is to get you thinking about your business differently than you have before. Here's a quick recap:

1. There is still time for you to carve out your niche online, to build a business around it and get very wealthy, but it's not going to last that much longer.
2. In order to have a real business you must have a vision and create a strategy to achieve that vision. And if you do this you'll leave the opportunity seeker world and enter the world of the entrepreneur.
3. Stop going around collecting tactics and only buy products and services that will support your strategy in achieving your vision.

4. Realize that your time is all you have therefore you need to know its current value and have a plan to increase it.
5. Always remember you need to build a business around scalability and leverage.
6. Know the difference between out-tasking and outsourcing and build a network of relationships, so you have access to talented freelancers whenever you need them.
7. Study and use project management methodologies to grow your business.
8. Process map your way of doing things and seek to continually improve your processes.
9. Attempt to reduce every activity and relationship down to a core metric that makes it easy for you to gauge performance.

If you follow these suggestions you'll be well on your way to increasing your income while reducing your stress and work hours.

Skyrocket The Results Of Your Business

As I mentioned at the beginning of this manifesto I have entered into a partnership that's causing me to adjust my coaching timeline. In 2009 I will be partnering with Agora Publishing in the creation of a hybrid coaching and consulting business that will be geared towards bigger and more established businesses with a much higher price tag associated to it. Our projections show that this new program will take the majority of my time and therefore new clients to my coaching program will no longer get the opportunity to work with me personally.

In order to complete the systemization of my coaching program I've decided to offer my personal coaching one last time in an intensive 11 month program. You'll have the opportunity to make gains in just eleven months that other people took several years to implement.

This program is certainly not for everyone, it will be intense and we will be working very closely together. Since each client will have the opportunity to work with me directly during our weekly group coaching calls, the program will have a very real limit on the number of people accepted and it won't be sold at bargain basement prices either.

Make More Money, More Often, With Less Effort

So, it adds up to this:

In my business coaching program, I'll be sharing the strategies currently being used by people at the top of the Internet marketing world.

I can promise you these are not concepts you've heard before but they have one thing in common; they are *so* powerful they will increase your business even if you do them wrong!

To register for this program right now before it fills up, visit:
http://www.strategicprofits.com/IBMcoaching/

Stay Tuned,

Rich Schefren